3 0400 00521 216 8

AIRDRIE

D0549061

For Abigail Bethan, Joseph David, and Amy Faith,
from their grandmother's old school friend
—M. H.

For little Charlie Uberoi, our miracle in New York
—C. B.

Henry Holt and Company, LLC
Publishers since 1866
175 Fifth Avenue
New York, New York 10010
www.HenryHoltKids.com

Henry Holt® is a registered trademark of Henry Holt and Company, LLC.
Kings and Queens of the Bible copyright © 2008 by Frances Lincoln Limited
Text copyright © 2008 by Mary Hoffman
Illustrations copyright © 2008 by Christina Balit
All rights reserved.
First published in the United States in 2008 by Henry Holt and Company, LLC.
Distributed in Canada by H. B. Fenn and Company Ltd.
Simultaneously published in Great Britain in 2008 by Frances Lincoln Limited

Library of Congress Cataloging-in-Publication Data
Hoffman, Mary.
Kings and queens of the Bible / by Mary Hoffman ; illustrated by Christina Balit.
p.   cm.
1. Kings and rulers—Biblical teaching—Juvenile literature. 2. Queens in the Bible—Juvenile literature.
I. Balit, Christina, ill. II. Title.
BS1199.K5H64   2007   220.9′2—dc22   2007042256

ISBN-13: 978-0-8050-8837-3 / ISBN-10: 0-8050-8837-7
First American Edition—2008
The artist used watercolor, gouache, gold inks, and pencils to create the illustrations for this book.
Printed in China on acid-free paper. ∞

1 3 5 7 9 10 8 6 4 2

MARIGOLD LIBRARY SYSTEM

KINGS AND QUEENS
OF THE BIBLE

MARY HOFFMAN

Illustrated by

CHRISTINA BALIT

HENRY HOLT AND COMPANY

NEW YORK

AIRDRIE MUNICIPAL LIBRARY
Bay 111, 304 Main Street S
Airdrie, AB T4B 3C3

INTRODUCTION

The Old Testament is full of kings and queens, vivid characters who play an important part in the history of the people who came to be called the Jews.

Some were kings who treated the Jews as slaves, such as the pharaoh of Egypt or King Belshazzar of Babylon. Some were rulers selected by God from among the Chosen People, such as Saul and David.

All the Jews were descendants of the twelve sons of Jacob, who was given the extra name "Israel" by God. Israel was the grandson of Abraham, the man appointed by God to lead His people, and eventually those people were all known by the grandson's name: Israelites.

Jacob's most famous son was Joseph, who interpreted strange dreams for one of the pharaohs of Egypt, and whose brothers joined him there. After many generations of exile in Egypt, the Israelites followed a new leader, Moses, through the desert for forty years in search of a Promised Land filled with milk and honey.

When they settled, in the lands around the river Jordan, the twelve tribes had their own territory in a united Israel. But after the death of King Solomon the kingdom was divided and eventually lost.

But before then there were the kings and queens you can read about in this book—some wise, some brave, some bloodthirsty, some promise-breaking, some greedy, some righteous—and all of them larger than life.

Mary M Hoffman

CONTENTS

PHARAOH AND MOSES

The ancient Egyptians called their king *pharaoh*, which means "great house." And the Egyptian rulers did come from great houses—their families ruled for thousands of years. We can still see the pyramids today, built as spectacular tombs for the most important pharaohs.

Several kings of Egypt feature in the Bible, and their stories became entangled with the history of the Israelites, the Jewish people of the Old Testament.

Hundreds of years after Joseph and his brothers had died in Egypt, many generations of Jews had descended from them, and there was an Israelite leader called Moses.

During the reign of the pharaoh who ruled Egypt at the time of Moses, the Israelites were treated as slaves. They were desperate and looked for someone to lead them out of Egypt to a better life.

Moses had been special from birth. Born to an Israelite couple, he had been raised by an Egyptian princess. And when he grew up, he heard the voice of God speaking to him from a burning bush. God told him to ask Pharaoh to let the Israelites go.

"Hmm," thought Pharaoh. "If I let them go they will never come back. And then what would I do for slaves?"

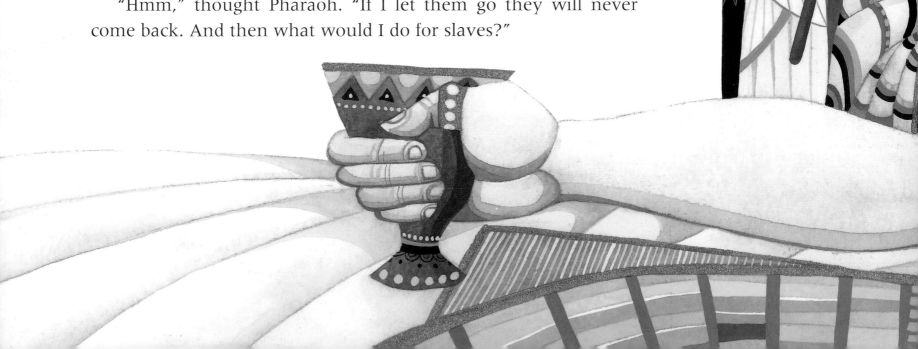

So instead he worked the Israelite slaves even harder and had them beaten even more brutally. Moses spoke to God, and God decided to frighten Pharaoh into obeying His will.

The first thing that happened was that the river Nile ran with blood instead of water. Just imagine, no water to drink or bathe in or for plants—only blood!

Eight more plagues followed. There were swarms of frogs, lice, flies, and locusts; and boils broke out on all the Egyptian people and animals. The cattle were diseased; there was hail with thunder and fire; and then there was a terrible darkness that lasted for three whole days and nights. And still Pharaoh would not let the Israelites go.

Then came the worst plague of all: the death of all the Egyptians' firstborn, including the king's own son and heir. But the Israelites were unharmed. They had put a mark on their doors, and the Angel of Death had passed over them. That is the origin of the Jewish feast of Passover.

Pharaoh was so grief-stricken at the death of his son that at last he agreed to let the Israelites go. But, as soon as they left, he changed his mind and sent a huge army after them.

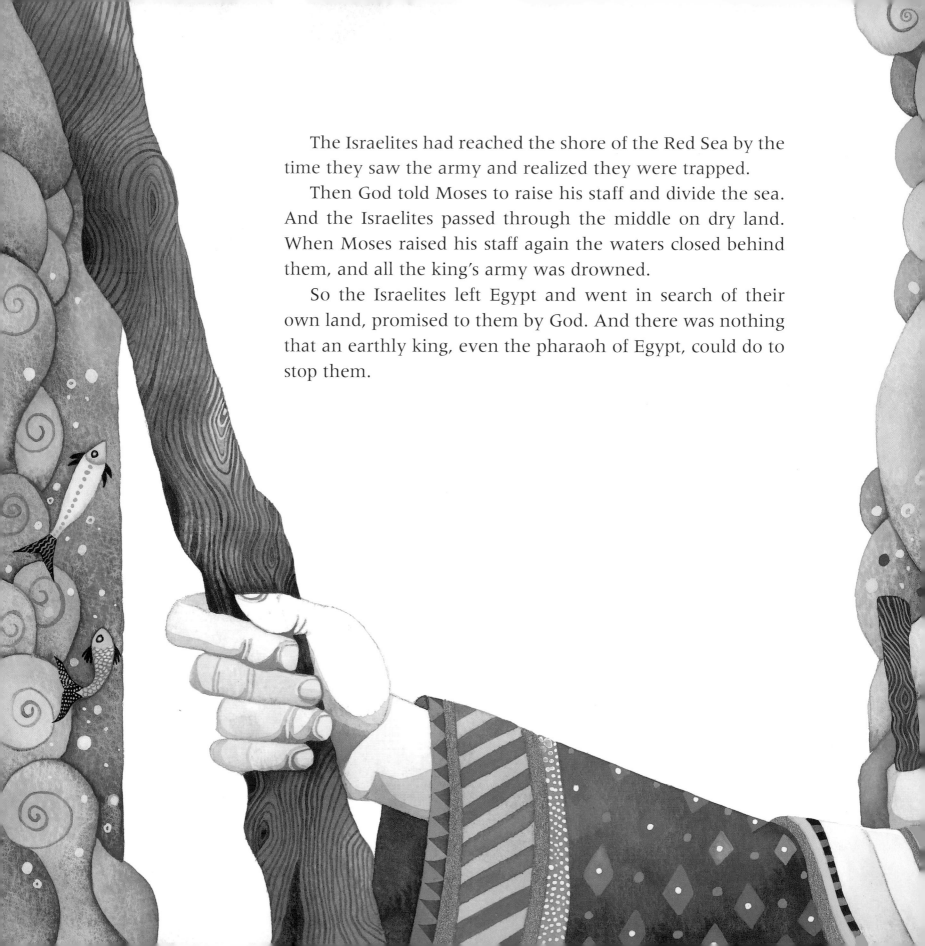

The Israelites had reached the shore of the Red Sea by the time they saw the army and realized they were trapped.

Then God told Moses to raise his staff and divide the sea. And the Israelites passed through the middle on dry land. When Moses raised his staff again the waters closed behind them, and all the king's army was drowned.

So the Israelites left Egypt and went in search of their own land, promised to them by God. And there was nothing that an earthly king, even the pharaoh of Egypt, could do to stop them.

KING DAVID

The Israelites eventually settled in Canaan, and a piece of land was given to each of the twelve tribes, named after the twelve sons of Jacob. The whole country was called Israel and was ruled over by judges instead of kings. The last and greatest of these was the prophet Samuel. But the Israelites did not like Samuel's son and wanted to have a king again.

Samuel first chose a king of the Israelites called Saul. But God was not pleased with King Saul. So He sent Samuel to the house of a man called Jesse, in Bethlehem, saying that he would find a new king among Jesse's sons.

Now, Jesse had lots of sons. Samuel went to see them but none seemed quite right, even though each was a fine-looking young man.

"Do you have any more sons?" he asked Jesse.

"Well, there's young David," said Jesse. "But he is out in the fields looking after the sheep."

Samuel told Jesse to send for David. When David came, the prophet saw straightaway that this was the one, so he anointed young David's head with oil, which meant he would be the next king.

As well as being a shepherd, David was a musician who played for King Saul. He also wrote some of the Psalms you can read in the Bible today. But he didn't become king for a long time. He went back to looking after his father's sheep.

Then the Philistines declared war on Israel. All David's older brothers went into the army, but he stayed behind on his father's farm.

The Philistines sent their champion to frighten the Israelites. He was a great giant of a man called Goliath, and he was a terrifying sight. He roared out a challenge for the Israelites to send a champion from their army to meet him in single combat.

None of the Israelites dared to face him.

One day, David was taking some food to his brothers in the army. "Who is that?" he asked when he saw Goliath strutting up and down.

"That's the Philistine champion," they told him. "Whoever kills him will have the king's daughter for a wife and a fortune in gold."

"I'll do it," said David, but everyone laughed at him because he was only a boy. In fact, he was too small for any of the armor he was offered. Instead, he went down to a brook and chose five smooth stones, which he put in his bag. He had his slingshot with him, and armed with only the sling and his stones, he went out to face the giant.

Goliath sneered when he saw the Israelites' champion. "Come on, then!" he said. "I shall feed your body to the birds of the air and the beasts of the field."

David said, "You come armed with spear and sword, but I come in the name of the Lord. Today I shall kill you, to show that the God of Israel is the winner in this battle."

Then David took his sling and shot one of the pebbles straight at Goliath's face. It hit him between the eyes—the only place where he had no armor—and Goliath fell to the ground. David ran up, took hold of Goliath's sword, and struck off the giant's head.

After this, David lived at King Saul's palace and became great friends with his son Jonathan. The two young men were inseparable and promised to stay friends forever. David married Jonathan's sister Michal and became one of King Saul's most successful generals.

King Saul tried to turn Jonathan against his friend, saying, "You will never be king as long as David lives." But Jonathan sent a message to David telling him to hide from the king, and that kept him safe.

After Saul died, David became king, though at first only over Judah, the southern part of the kingdom. Later he was king of the whole country. He made Jerusalem his capital, which is why it is sometimes called the City of David.

David was king for forty years and he had many wives and children. He brought the Ark of the Israelites, their most sacred object, to Jerusalem, where he wanted to build a temple to put it in. He consulted a prophet named Nathan about this, but Nathan said that the temple would be built by David's son, not by David himself.

After David died, he was buried in his own city, Jerusalem, and his son Solomon became king after him.

KING SOLOMON

God appeared to Solomon in a dream and said, "Ask me for whatever you like and I shall give it to you."

King Solomon thought for a bit and then said, "Lord, give me wisdom, so that I can tell the difference between good and evil and be a good king to Your people."

God was very pleased. "You could have asked for great riches or a long life or for the death of your enemies. But you chose wisdom and, because of that, I shall give you wealth and long life, too."

Throughout King Solomon's reign, the country of Israel prospered and the people had better lives than they had ever had before or would ever have again.

There are many stories about how wise King Solomon was, but the most famous is that of a baby boy who was claimed by two women.

These two women had both given birth to sons on the same night. In the morning one of the babies was found dead and the other was alive and well. Both women claimed that the remaining baby was her son and they were brought before the king so that he could decide the case.

"Fetch me a sword," the king said to one of his servants. "Since they both claim the boy, the only thing to do is to cut him in two and give them half each."

"Oh no!" cried one woman. "Don't hurt him. Let her have him rather than kill him."

The other woman just shrugged.

"Give the baby to the first woman," said the king. "Since she loves him enough to give him up rather than see him hurt, she is the real mother."

It was Solomon who carried out David's plan to build a temple, and it became famous throughout the world.

The temple was made of stone and cedar wood, and the outside was covered with gold. At the heart of the temple was a place called the Holy of Holies, where King David wanted to place the Ark that the Israelites had brought with them out of Egypt. It was a box containing two stone tablets with the Ten Commandments written on them.

There were two angels made of olive wood to guard the Ark, and the Holy of Holies was such a sacred place that no one was allowed in it, except, once a year, the high priest.

In front of the temple were two bronze pillars decorated with pomegranates and a bronze altar resting on the back of twelve bronze bulls, representing the twelve tribes of Israel. When the temple was finished, Solomon dedicated it to God and God promised that there would always be a king in Israel as long as the temple lasted and the people stayed faithful to Him.

King Solomon ruled for forty years and had many wives and children. But he forgot his promises to God and started to worship some of the gods his wives believed in, like the goddess Astarte. His great wisdom did not save him from that foolishness. So when King Solomon died, God caused the kingdom to be divided. The ten tribes in the north called their land Israel, and the two in the south—Judah and Benjamin—called their land Judah. And in time, because of this, the people of Judah became known as Jews.

THE QUEEN OF SHEBA

Rumors of the wealth and wisdom of King Solomon spread far and wide in his lifetime. They reached as far as Sheba, in southwest Arabia, which was ruled by a queen who was also famous for her wisdom.

Balkis was her name, and she decided to pay the great king of Israel a royal visit. She set out for Jerusalem with a train of camels laden with presents for Solomon—enough gold to weigh nine thousand pounds!

And that was not all she had in her luggage. There were precious stones—rubies, emeralds, and diamonds—and a great quantity of spices, more than the Israelites had seen before or since. There was cinnamon and mace, cassia and cloves, saffron and poppy seed, tamarind and pomegranate, nutmeg and ginger, coriander and cumin, and even the root of balsam, which produced precious healing oil.

Never had anyone given such costly gifts to the king, and he was mightily pleased with them. But the first thing Queen Balkis did when the two rulers met was to ask Solomon some difficult questions. After all, she was as interested in his wisdom as his wealth.

The Bible doesn't tell us what the questions were, but they were probably riddles because it was considered very wise to be able to solve such puzzles. Solomon did very well and solved all the riddles the Queen of Sheba could think of, and she was quite impressed.

She was also impressed by King Solomon's house and the rich livery of his servants and by what she saw of his great temple. At the end of the visit, she said, "I had heard much about you, but the reports didn't tell me even half the truth. Your people are lucky indeed to be ruled by such a wise king, and I envy your wives for having such a rich and clever husband."

You might have thought that there would be a marriage between King Solomon and Queen Balkis of Sheba but, although there are some legends that they had a child together, the Bible says that after exchanging their fabulous gifts, the Queen of Sheba gathered her people and went back to her own country.

QUEEN JEZEBEL

About fifty years after the death of King Solomon, Ahab became ruler of the Northern Kingdom of Israel. He was one of the worst kings his people ever had, but his wife, Queen Jezebel, was even more wicked.

Jezebel was a Phoenician princess who worshipped Baal, the god of rain and storms. Hers was a cruel religion, which called for the sacrifice of children, and she persuaded King Ahab to follow it, too.

King Ahab was greedy, and Jezebel encouraged his greed. There was a man called Naboth, who had a vineyard beside the royal palace, which Ahab wanted for himself.

"Let me have your vineyard, Naboth," the king said, "because it is so convenient for my palace and I want to grow vegetables there. I shall give you another vineyard somewhere else or, if you prefer, I shall pay you good money for it."

But Naboth didn't want to let the king have his vineyard because he had inherited it from his father. So Ahab went grumbling to his wife about it.

"Are you the king of Israel or not?" said Queen Jezebel. "I'll see to it that the vineyard shall be yours."

And she wrote some letters, signed with the king's seal, which arranged for two wicked men to come and accuse Naboth of saying bad things about God and the king. The punishment for that crime was death by stoning. And, although Naboth was completely innocent, he was stoned to death.

"Now you can take Naboth's vineyard," said the queen.

There was a powerful prophet in Israel called Elijah, and God sent him to the king and queen.

"Because of what you have done," Elijah told Ahab, "you shall die and dogs shall drink your blood. And as for your queen, Jezebel, the dogs shall eat her body."

King Ahab died in battle, and a few years passed before Jezebel received her punishment. Jehu, a general, had been anointed king of Israel and he shot Ahab's son, Jehoram, with an arrow, in the very place where Naboth's vineyard had been.

Then Jehu went to the house where Queen Jezebel was. She put on her best clothes and jewels and lots of makeup and sat in the window, thinking that she would impress Jehu with her finery. But he called up to her servants and said, "Who will throw her down?"

Her servants willingly threw her out of the window!

She fell, and Jehu's horses trampled her body. Jehu said to his servants, "You had better bury the body of Jezebel, since she was the daughter of a king."

But they found only her skull and her feet and the palms of her hands; the rest had been eaten by dogs. When they reported this, Jehu said, "Elijah's prophecy has come to pass."

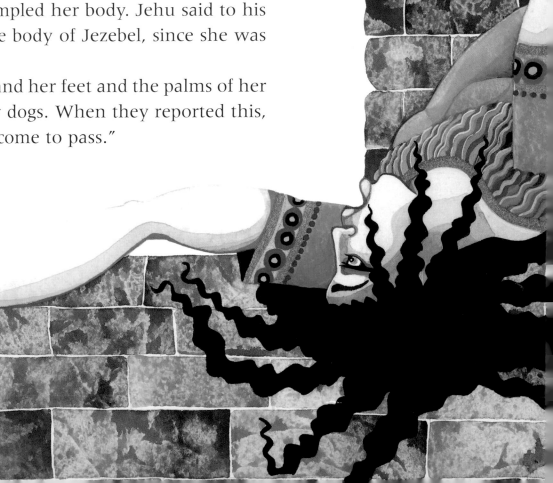

King Belshazzar

More generations passed and the Israelites gradually forgot God and started to worship other gods. So the two kingdoms were destroyed and the temple at Jerusalem lay in ruins. And the people were carried off to be slaves in Babylon, which was the capital city of a mighty empire.

King Belshazzar gave a great feast in Babylon and invited a thousand nobles to it. When he was quite drunk, the king called for his servants to bring out the grandest drinking cups he possessed.

The trouble was that these gold and silver vessels had been stolen from the temple at Jerusalem by Belshazzar's father. These were vessels sacred to the Israelites, and here was the drunken Babylonian king swigging wine out of them! Not just him, but his lords, his wives, and other women of the court. And as they drank, they sang praises to their pagan gods of gold, silver, bronze, iron, wood, and stone.

Then and there, in the middle of the feast, a disembodied hand appeared and began to write a message on the wall of the banquet hall, beside the king's candlestick. And these were the words it wrote:

MENE, MENE, TEKEL, UPHARSIN.

Nobody could make anything of this, least of all King Belshazzar. But he was very frightened by the ghostly hand and its mysterious message. So he decided to offer a reward of a gold chain and a powerful position in his court to anyone who could tell him what it meant.

The queen, who was Belshazzar's mother, reminded him that his father had a man called Daniel in his court who was famous for interpreting dreams. So the king called for Daniel and offered him the reward.

"You can keep your gold chain and your position of power," said Daniel, who cared nothing for the importance of kings. "But I'll tell you what the message means. It came straight from God and it means, 'The days of your kingdom are at an end. You have been weighed in the balance and found wanting. Your kingdom will be divided and given to the Medes and Persians.'"

The king didn't like what he had been told, but he ordered the gold chain to be put round Daniel's neck and a purple robe given him to wear. And he proclaimed Daniel to be the third most important man in the kingdom.

That same night King Belshazzar was murdered. And his kingdom was taken over by Darius the Mede.

Queen Esther

There was a Jew in Persia called Mordecai, who was a descendant of the tribe of Benjamin and a very distant relative of King Saul's. Mordecai reared his orphaned cousin as his own daughter and she was very beautiful. Hadassah was her Jewish name, but she was also known as Esther.

Ahasuerus was king of the Persians at this time, many hundreds of years after the death of Belshazzar. But the Jews were still being persecuted. Ahasuerus ruled in the city of Susa and, in the third year of his reign, he was looking for a wife.

Esther was one of the young women chosen to be brought before Ahasuerus. She lived with the other girls in the king's palace for a year, being further enhanced with scented oils and expensive ointments. During all that time, the king never saw her. But when he did, he chose Esther to be his most important wife and his queen, and he placed the crown on her head.

Esther had a secret. She had told no one at the palace that she was Jewish. Soon after she became queen, her adopted father, Mordecai, discovered a plot to kill the king. He told Esther and she told the king and the plot was foiled.

Then the king appointed a man called Haman to be his second in command. This Haman hated the Jews. He particularly hated Mordecai, who would never bow to him. So Haman and his wife plotted to kill Mordecai and had a great wooden gallows built on which to hang him.

Queen Esther prepared a banquet for the king and Haman and entertained them charmingly. Haman thought what a very fine fellow he was, dining with the king and queen. But it irked him to see Mordecai still alive. During the banquet the king remembered that Mordecai had done him a favor and asked Haman, "What should be given to a man who has done his king a good service?"

Haman, thinking that the king meant him, said, "Oh, sire, he should be given a robe that the king has worn and a horse that the king has ridden—with a royal crown on its head—and the man should be clothed in the robe and set on the horse and led through the city while heralds proclaim, 'Here is a man that the king wants to honor!'"

"Let it be done," said Ahasuerus. "Take the robe and the horse to Mordecai."

Airdrie Municipal Library

And, if that was not enough, Esther revealed to the king that she was a Jew and that her people were being persecuted by Haman.

The king was so much in love with Esther and so angry with Haman that he had him hanged on the gallows that had been prepared for Mordecai. And he appointed Mordecai in Haman's place.

After that, Esther used her influence to reverse all Haman's plans for killing the Jews. She and Mordecai instituted the feast of Purim, when people sent each other gifts of food and gave presents to the poor. And to this day, in honor of what Queen Esther did for them, Jews celebrate the feast of Purim every year.

About the Kings and Queens

Pharaoh and Moses

There is not space enough here to tell of all that Moses did in Egypt, or the full details of the plagues. But all these stories are told in the book of Exodus and can be read there.

King David

The story of Samuel choosing David is in 1 Samuel 15–16. In the Bible version, Jesse has eight sons, but there is another tradition that David was the seventh, making him the seventh son of a seventh son—always a magical position. The other stories of David are in the two books of Samuel.

King Solomon

Stories of Solomon can be found in the first book of Kings.

The Queen of Sheba

This story is found in 1 Kings 10 and 2 Chronicles 9. Sheba used to be identified with Saba, a country in the southwest of Arabia, roughly where Yemen is today. Modern scholars think it might have been farther north but admit that it makes the fabled voyage of its queen less romantic. The name Balkis, or Bilkis, is not used in the Bible but comes from Arabic tradition. (In the form Balkis it is also used by Kipling in "The Butterfly That Stamped" in his *Just So Stories*.) The legend about the child of Solomon and the queen says that he might have been King Nebuchadnezzar.

Queen Jezebel

The bloodthirsty story of the queen's death can be found in the second book of Kings, chapter 9. The story of Naboth's vineyard and his death is told in 1 Kings 21.

King Belshazzar

The famous story of King Belshazzar and the writing on the wall can be found in Daniel 5. Daniel is the man who was thrown into the lions' den. Some traditions hold that the Hebrew writing on the wall was written from top to bottom, as in the picture. There is controversy about the actual identity of Belshazzar's successor, since Babylon was captured by Cyrus the Great of Persia and not by the Medes.

Queen Esther

Esther is one of only two women to have a book of the Bible named after her (the other is Ruth). The name Esther is a variant of Ishtar, the Babylonian goddess. Her Jewish name, Hadassah, means "myrtle." Ahasuerus has been identified as both Xerxes I (486–465 BCE) and as Artaxerxes II (405–359 BCE). The reason he wanted a new wife was that Queen Vashti had defied him at a banquet when he commanded her to come to him. The feast of Purim is celebrated in March or April.

Airdrie Municipal Library